Using ICT

DEVELOPING ADULT TEACHING AND LEARNING: PRACTITIONER GUIDES

Barbara Nance, Maria Kambouri and Harvey Mellar

niace
promoting adult learning

(England and Wales)
21 De Montfort Street
Leicester LE1 7GE`

Company registration no. 2603322
Charity registration no. 1002775
Published by NIACE in association with NRDC.

NIACE has a broad remit to promote lifelong learning opportunities for adults.
NIACE works to develop increased participation in education and training,
particularly for those who do not have easy access because of class, gender, age,
race, language and culture, learning difficulties or disabilities, or insufficient
financial resources.

For a full catalogue of all NIACE's publications visit
www.niace.org.uk/publications

Cataloguing in Publications Data
A CIP record for this title is available from the British Library
ISBN 978-1-86201-338-4

Cover design by Creative by Design Limited, Paisley
Designed and typeset by Creative by Design Limited, Paisley
Printed and bound by Aspect Binders and Print Ltd

Developing adult teaching and learning: Practitioner guides

This is one of several linked publications arising from the five Effective Practice Studies carried out by the National Research and Development Centre for Adult Literacy and Numeracy (NRDC) from 2003 to 2007.

The five studies explored effective teaching and learning in reading, writing, numeracy, ESOL and using ICT. To date, three series of publications have been produced from the Effective Practice Studies: the research reports and the development project reports, all published by NRDC; and these practitioner guides, published in partnership between NIACE and NRDC.

For more information on the first two series, please see **www.nrdc.org.uk**

Contents

Acknowledgements

The authors would like to thank the following people for their contribution to this publication:

The researcher-practitioners for all their insights, hard work, enthusiasm and good humour:

- John Budis
- Elizabeth Caush
- Cathy Clarkson
- Maggie Cochran
- Jo Dixon
- Steve Harris
- Graciano Soares
- Jenny Wilkes

Their 'buddies':

- Wojciech Dmochowski
- Mo Francis
- Muzammil Haque
- Rowan Harris
- Frieda Marti-Collet
- Sandy Metcalf
- Sue Smith

The practitioners who wrote the case studies:

- Sally Betts
- John Budis
- Maggie Cochran
- Jo Dixon
- Frieda Marti-Collett

Peer review

This guide was peer reviewed. The critical readers were:

- Wojciech Dmochowski
- Kevin Donovan
- Judith Hinman
- Vanessa Hooper

About this guide

This guide shows how digital technologies can be used to enhance teaching and learning in *Skills for Life* provision. It provides practitioners with practical tips and ideas for using ICT in their teaching. These ideas can be transferred within different curriculum areas and teaching contexts.

Based on a research and development project on the use of ICT in effective teaching and learning (Mellar *et al.*, 2007), we present several teaching approaches that have been proposed and trialled by tutors working on this project using digital technologies with *Skills for Life* learners in literacy, numeracy and ESOL. Examples are given by way of seven case studies, in order to motivate the use of different technologies in similar contexts and give sufficient information to allow tutors to start using a particular approach.

These teaching approaches are based on four guiding principles, which came out of the first phase of our study: *collaboration, autonomy,* technology diversity or *variety* and construction of *artefacts.* These principles are explained in Section 1.

1 | **Background**

The ICT Effective Teaching and Learning Study

The aim of this research project was to develop effective ICT-based teaching strategies through a series of trials using theoretically grounded ICT task designs targeted at specific adult literacy and ESOL learning objectives. We examined both the development of literacy skills through the use of ICT, and the development of ICT skills.

Working with nine tutors who agreed to participate as practitioner-researchers, we developed 14 teaching interventions based on schemes of work that both embedded ICT literacy within LLN classes and introduced pedagogical techniques such as small group work.

Involvement of tutors was a key element, both in deciding on the development of the ICT interventions and in the research process through reflection on their developing practice using ICT. The tutors were interviewed and observed, and the learners were assessed at the start and end of their course for attainment in reading and listening in English using standard tests as well as attitude and attainment in ICT literacy through bespoke questionnaires and assessment materials matched to the *Skills for Life* ICT curriculum.

It is this practice, resulting from a year's development work, that tutors were invited to illustrate in this guide by way of case studies.

At the core of the approach to learning and teaching that we adopted is the creation of 'learning opportunities', as described by Ivanič and Tseng (2005):

> *Classroom interaction is, as noted in many studies (...), a means of transforming the content which a teacher plans to convey into knowledge and skills available for learning, through the co-production of learning opportunities. Interaction provides learners with opportunities to absorb knowledge from input, to practise the skills taught in class or to modify or polish learning strategies. The value of the concept of 'learning opportunities' is that it does not imply that what a teacher plans to convey is the same as what a learner gains from a lesson.*

In developing this framework and the core concept of learning opportunities, we derived four guiding design principles. While all of these need not be present all of the time, they always guided our designs.

The four guiding principles

Collaboration

Flexibility in classroom management is key: accepting collaboration when it occurs naturally, fostering peer collaboration through joint tasks, directing learners to specific reinforcement activities if necessary, and sometimes avoiding intervention as part of a process of encouraging independence.

Autonomy

Promoting self-directed learning with *Skills for Life* learners was strongly encouraged, and the tutors were seen to move from a view of the tutor as expert to a view of the tutor as facilitator and supporter of the development of autonomous learners.

Variety

The ability of ICT to motivate adult learners, both to enter learning and to stick with it, has often been discussed (Mellar *et al.*, 2001; Kambouri *et al.*, 2003; Mellar *et al.*, 2004). However, 'traditional' digital technologies, such as the desktop computer, may well be losing their appeal; we were therefore keen to explore the motivational impact of a variety of technologies, such as mobile phones, tablets and digital video. The use of a wide range of up-to-date technologies might be motivational for adults, and the use of mobile technologies may have particular importance for adult learners. So we strove to incorporate a variety of technologies but also a variety of teaching strategies.

Support for the importance of the idea of variety of approaches is also found in the ESOL Effective Practice study:

> Teaching strategies that promoted balance and variety correlated with gains on test scores. These strategies balanced fluency and accuracy with a variety of activities and materials that keep learners engaged. The importance of balance and variety is underlined by the finding that learners performed best on the grammar and vocabulary sub-component of the test when they were taught neither too much nor too little grammar and vocabulary.
>
> (See **http://www.nrdc.org.uk/content.asp?CategoryID=1107**)

Artefacts

The use of technology to construct artefacts which allow learners to experiment was encouraged throughout this study. Evidence from the classroom indicates that this is often a useful focus, generating motivation, collaboration and purposeful action. It also enables ICT to be a tool in allowing differentiation in the classroom. In certain cases, role-play is also an important part of these activities, for instance when learners present themselves as journalists or TV interviewers.

2 | M-learning

What is M-learning?

M-learning, or mobile learning, uses technologies such as camera phones, handheld computers (PDAs), iPods and pocket games platforms. Here we focus on camera phones, most of which can be exploited for learning in many ways using such features as:

- text messaging;
- voice calls;
- taking and sharing photos, audio and video clips;
- sending multimedia messages to another device or a website;
- connecting to a computer to transfer files;
- installing and running software and games.

Why use M-learning?

Most learners, and particularly young adults, are familiar with mobile phones, which makes them a useful tool for exploring methods of teaching and learning.

Mobile phones are:

- easier to carry than laptops or tablet PCs, and often have sufficient computing power for data-capture tasks;
- easy to pass around, providing opportunities for interactions between learners;
- a stepping stone to computers;
- useful for learning at times and in places when a laptop or textbooks would be impractical;
- familiar and popular, especially among young adults;
- a means of making contact outside the classroom – e.g. text messaging for homework reminders and learning tips;
- useful on field trips, enabling learners to separate while remaining in contact with their tutor or each other.

How can M-learning be used?

- Private, personalised learning;

- non-threatening, informal assessment (e.g. games and quizzes);

- engaging new learners;

- using text messaging to work on writing and spelling, starting with the language learners are familiar with;

- taking, sharing and publishing photos as a starting point for engaging with language and numeracy;

- treasure hunt activities in which learners race to answer questions using clues in their environment;

- creating a 'mob-log' – taking photos, recording audio, making notes and publishing instantly on a website.

Case study: Using M-Learning with ESOL learners

Jo Dixon

Learners: ESOL all levels
Organisation: City College, Southampton
Technology: Camera phones and mediaBoard website (subscription required: see http://www.m-learning.org for details).

CASE STUDY

Aim: To use technology to bring language from the outside world into the classroom and use authentic examples to explore language and stimulate language production.

Background

The ESOL department at City College, Southampton, caters for people from a diverse range of ethnic and linguistic backgrounds learning English from Entry 1 through to Level 2. Four classes at different levels participated.

Mobile camera phones were used for a variety of mini-projects, most of which took between three and five 2-hour sessions to complete. The devices were used to record voices and take photos, which were sent as multimedia messages to a website. The site was further developed using a computer.

Using mobile technology

MediaBoard was used for most of the activities. This web-based tool creates a webpage that can be updated by text messages, pictures and audio sent from a mobile. MediaBoard is not unique in allowing users to create websites in this way, but it does have some unique features:

- The tutor registers the phone numbers of the phones the learners are using and can then message participants from the website.
- An image (e.g. a map or timeline) can be uploaded as the background for a webpage, and images and texts can be positioned on it.

Activities used the following format:

- researching or learning about a topic and analysing a particular language structure used in texts about it (e.g. on the Internet or in a museum)
- leaving the classroom and gathering pictures and information about the topic to populate a mediaBoard;
- developing and presenting the information on the mediaBoard.

Planned activities included:

- virtually 'meeting' a similar class in Australia, sharing photos and information on a world map, then showing them around our learning environment;
- interviewing staff about their jobs and writing texts to accompany photos and audio clips on a map of the campus;
- visiting museums and presenting information about local history on a timeline;
- reading about the Titanic, walking the city's Titanic Trail and reproducing it in photos on a map;
- studying the language of photo captions, then creating a 'moblog' – an online photo diary – of the college Open Day and allowing visitors to view pictures of events on the website almost instantly.

Projects covered a variety of language and ICT skills, but learners were able to use the other activities to focus on skills that were important to them.

Extract from session plan.

Date/Lesson ref.	Aims and objectives/ Learning outcomes	Student learning activities	Teaching methods	Resources	Key/Basic skills
17 June	Be ready to talk to people and create a weblog at the Open Day.	Practise asking for permission, asking questions to obtain information for captions; practise writing captions from information obtained. Look at the schedule for Open Day and decide who is responsible for what.	Teacher-led discussion and paired practical work.	Camera phones; copies of Open Day schedule.	Speak clearly in a way that suits the situation: Sc/L1.1a, Sc/L1.1c; make requests: Sc/L1.2a; write using complex sentences: Ws/E3.1a, Ws/L1.1a; use a range of noun and participle constructions: Ws/L2.1a.
19 June	Create a weblog of the Open day.	Attend part of Open Day and use skills learnt to create photo diary of it on the web.	Independent work in pairs or individually as preferred; teacher on hand to support and trouble-shoot.	Camera phones; get moblog site up on computers for visitors to view.	Speak clearly in a way that suits the situation: Sc/L1.1a, Sc/L1.1c; make requests: Sc/L1.2a; write using complex sentences: Ws/E3.1a, Ws/L1.1a; use a range of noun and participle constructions: Ws/L2.1a.
24 June	Evaluate project and learning.	View website of Open Day; edit and add captions if necessary. Post-project language assessment and self-reports.	Work individually or in pairs on captions; group discussion about project; individual assessment and self-assessment.	Assessment on network; ILPs.	ICT vocabulary: Rw/E3.1a; be aware of linguistic features that characterise different text types: Rs/l1.1a; write using complex sentences: Ws/E3.1a, Ws/L1.1a; use a range of noun and participle constructions: Ws/L2.1a.

Findings

New technologies

The project was met with great enthusiasm from learners. Using picture messaging for activities around the campus meant that the tutor could monitor pictures arriving on the website while maintaining contact with learners. This aspect of the technology would also lend itself to games such as treasure hunts.

Older learners and learners with disabilities

Amongst the learners were an older woman who initially expressed concern about handling a small device, and a visually impaired learner who was unable to see the screen. By the end of the project, the older learner had revised her attitude to the technology and the visually impaired learner felt the experience would help her to follow the conversations of younger family members.

Adapting the projects for different levels

The idea of focusing on language structures occurring in authentic texts was more successful with the higher-level classes. At lower levels, it was difficult to find texts that did not contain distracting language. However, the collecting of audio clips and photos proved popular with all levels, and it was also easy to focus on different skills and abilities.

Managing and using mobile devices

Decisions need to be made about choice of mobiles: any camera phone is adequate, but devices with greater computing power offer more possibilities. Organisations also need to consider how the devices will be stored and charged.

Tutor experiences

We were amongst the first to try out mediaBoard, and using computer software with mobile phones created some initial technical problems. Often tutors found themselves in unfamiliar territory, but this led to huge gains in confidence in their own use of ICT.

Top tips

1. Being involved with projects like this provides opportunities to develop understanding of mobile technologies as well as teaching and ICT skills. It is well worth the time involved.

2. Allow learners to experiment and send a few personal messages as they learn to use new devices, so they have got this urge out of the way before they are asked to focus on the learning activity.

3. Always have a Plan B for those occasions when a connection is unavailable or a picture message mysteriously disappears.

Resources

- Internet-connected computers
- Camera phones
- Mob-log site set up to receive test pictures
- Handout for language activities
- Subscription to mediaBoard

Teaching strategies

Collaboration

Learners were encouraged to work in pairs or small groups. This technology was new to all learners, and the groups were good at taking turns and offering mutual support. As the project developed, so did peer support. During one session in which learners explored a website and answered questions about the language used, one pair decided that the learner with weaker IT skills would operate the computer to gain practice while the other focused on language. At other times, learners with stronger IT skills were nominated to carry out computer tasks in order not to slow down the group's language work.

Encouraging autonomy

Learners were not given step-by-step instructions on using the phones but encouraged to transfer existing knowledge and become independent learners. For example:

- the tutor displays cards showing icons and words learners may already be familiar with from their use of TVs and computers, and leads discussion about their meaning;
- the tutor gives out handsets and tells learners to work in pairs and try to turn the device on, activate the camera and take a picture.

Learners who quickly mastered these processes were encouraged to help others (or indeed did so themselves). In this supportive atmosphere, new learners were able to acquire skills as they went along.

Variety

The project uses a variety of technologies (mobile phones, PDAs and desktop computers) and the framework allows for a huge variety of work, both on communication/ numeracy skills and ICT skills.

Artefacts

Creation of artefacts such as a webpage and mob-log enabled learners to develop fluency and competency through goal-oriented interaction.

Each part of this project saw learners working towards the creation of a multimedia presentation of their work.

They looked at information on another college's website and analysed language structures for explaining and describing, before developing texts to accompany the photos of their own college.

Using technology to create their own artefact, and interacting with artefacts created by others, gave learners a chance to put what they had learned into practice.

Useful links

These are just a few of the websites that allow you to upload photos and add text (some are free or offer free trials – please check for up-to-date charges):

mediaBoard is the platform we used most: **http://portal.m-learning.org/ mboard.php**

Ploggle is easy to use, with some nice design features: **http://www.ploggle.com**

Moblog has a simple linear design: **http://www.moblog.co.uk**

With Bubbleshare you can create photo albums and add speech bubbles with written or audio captions: **http://www.bubbleshare.com**

Flickr allows you to upload photos and attach labels to images: **http://www.flickr.com**

The moblearn blog keeps you up to date with what is going on in the world of m-learning and sometimes contains useful practical tips: **http://moblearn.blogspot.com/index.html**

3 Mind mapping

What is mind mapping?

A mind map is a diagram which can help to present and arrange ideas relating to a central topic. Branches and sub branches connect the ideas. Colour and images are used to differentiate between the parts of the diagram, which uses spatial rather than linear organisation and visual techniques to help clarify students' thinking.

Why use it?

Electronic mind mapping has been shown to help dyslexic learners organise their ideas. Learners can brainstorm and create electronic mind maps as ideas occur. These ideas can then be moved around and grouped logically. Learners can easily make alterations, and the maps can be built up over time.

Electronic mind mapping contains a number of tools such as: ability to move ideas from one place to another, to edit ideas, to connect, to annotate, to promote and demote ideas within the hierarchy, to view branches of a map at various levels of detail, to link other documents, web sites etc. The spatial diagram can also be translated into linear form, providing a structure to write a letter or other text.

How can it be used?

- To organise ideas and thoughts prior to writing;
- for presentations;
- to create links to other documents and websites;
- for pictorial representation of ideas;
- to edit and move ideas around easily;
- to brainstorm ideas;
- to make notes;
- as a memory aid;
- to create session plans.

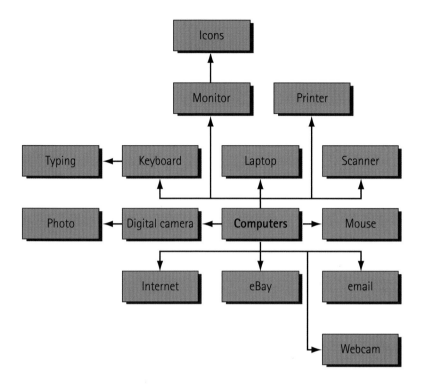

A mind map produced by learners.

Case study: Using electronic mind mapping with literacy groups

Maggie Cochran

Learners: Literacy Entry 2 – Level 1
Organisation: FE : St Vincent College, Gosport
Technology: Mind mapping software

Aim: To develop learners' planning skills using mind mapping software.

Background

This was a mixed – gender and age – class of 11 students, 10 with English as their first language. The course, called 'Starter Literacy on the Computer', ran for two hours a week over 12 weeks. Participants generally wanted to improve literacy skills while learning how to use a computer.

The mind mapping software used was *Inspiration.*

CASE STUDY

Using mind mapping with learners

Electronic mind mapping was integrated into a number of literacy-based activities to help learners organise their thoughts, plan their work and structure it into paragraphs. Exported into Word, the maps became a basis for writing. The tutor was keen to encourage peer support.

Using mind mapping software

As an introduction, the mind mapping application was demonstrated by modelling a brainstorming exercise that would normally have been put on to a flip chart. Learners were surprised at how easy it was to enter the information.

The students were then able to work in small groups, brainstorming the topic of computers. Each group worked around a computer taking turns to enter the information and record ideas. The groups worked well, with lots of relevant dialogue.

The groups worked at different paces: the tutor was able to spend time talking to them about their words and showing them how to organise their ideas into logical groupings.

The maps were printed out both in mind-map and linear format. The students were then able to use them as a structural aid as they worked individually on a word-processed article.

They were able to write three or more paragraphs each, with ideas logically sequenced. These articles were then illustrated with clip-art.

Inspiration software was also used to plan articles and for thinking about the format and content of formal letters.

Findings

Group work was key during these sessions. The learners worked well together, taking turns to enter information. The single ESOL learner in the class benefited from the language exchange. She had better IT skills than some older members of the class, and was allocated the task of using the mouse. This meant that she had to follow instructions in a real-life situation.

Learners became more comfortable asking for help from each other, offering suggestions and sharing expertise. They also contributed more to group discussions.

Lesson plan. Literacy – paragraph writing

Name: Location:

Time: 2 hours   Session:

Lesson objectives: To learn how to mind map to plan written work (Wt/L1.1 and Wt/L2.1)

Time	Tutor activities	Student activities	Teaching aids
10 minutes	Demonstrate using a computer-based mind map, e.g. Inspiration. Discuss creation of new idea boxes and links between ideas. Demonstrate how to move ideas around to form logical groupings.	Observe and contribute ideas.	Computer with mind mapping software.
10 minutes	Begin a mind map of 'the computer' on the whiteboard, eliciting ideas from students about subheadings they might want to branch to, e.g.: advantages, history, peripherals.	Contribute ideas to a shared mind map.	Whiteboard, pens.
40 minutes	Facilitate and offer guidance where required. Guide learners towards organising ideas into logical groupings.	Work in small groups to build mind maps of 'the computer'. Rearrange ideas into logical groupings. Print and save maps.	Work individually or in pairs on captions; group discussion about project; individual assessment and self-assessment.
10 minutes	Coffee break		
45 minutes	Discuss requirements for article – three paragraphs, based on ideas from mind map.	Work individually to write a short article about computers based on the mind mapped plan using Word. Save and print plan.	Computers with Word, printer.
5 minutes	Summarise and remind students to close down computers	Log off and shut down computers	

The mind mapping software helped students plan their work and focus their thinking. Word-processing then enabled them to produce a professional looking document. Learners were motivated, and the social interaction fostered an environment conducive to learning.

Taking a step back and adopting a facilitating role, the tutor had more time to observe her learners and find different ways to support their language development. Retention improved, with learners reluctant to miss sessions.

Top tips

1. Make time to explore all the functionality of the mind mapping software.
2. Make sure you and learners are clear on the aims of the task before starting.
3. Think about why you are using ICT – does it add anything to the lesson?
4. Use the groups' diversity to develop the chemistry of the group – the most unlikely groupings can produce surprising results.
5. Challenge your learners by asking open questions: e.g. 'What if?' or 'What do you think?'
6. Encourage learners to develop problem-solving skills by not instantly providing solutions.

Resources

- Computers with mind mapping software – one per group
- Mind mapping software: Inspiration **http://www.inspiration.com**
- Printer

Teaching strategies

Collaboration

Learners can find ICT-based classes a solitary experience. Here, the tutor encouraged social interaction and created a relaxed learning environment in which learners felt able to experiment, make mistakes and benefit from other people's ideas.

The use of mind mapping software opened up discussions, and the brainstorming exercise would not have worked nearly so well using pen and paper.

The classroom atmosphere seemed friendly as a result of the collaborative working. Learners were very supportive of each other and peer praise was a powerful factor in building confidence. They learned that there was not always a right answer and benefited from sharing experiences. The learners frequently arranged to meet outside the sessions to continue and reinforce learning.

Autonomy

As the learners became accustomed to working collaboratively, they were more inclined to seek peer assistance rather than wait for the tutor. Learners started to take responsibility for their learning. The tutor challenged her learners by asking open questions, encouraging them to develop problem-solving skills by not instantly providing solutions.

Learners also became less reliant on handouts, although they liked to have them for revision. They began to have more confidence in their own abilities as they realised they each had different strengths and skills.

Variety

The learners all seemed to be engaged and motivated by the variety of activity and working practice. They found the change in representation of the map into a linear format useful in providing a structure for their written work.

Artefacts

The learners produced printed mind maps, and used these as a basis for planning their articles. Although the maps were produced by learners working in small groups, their plans and articles were further developed individually.

Useful links

Case study: How mind mapping was used in teacher training:
   http://ferl.qia.org.uk/display.cfm?resID=3266

Using electronic mind maps in teaching:
   http://www.escalate.ac.uk/resources/mindmapsoftware/

4 Using Tablet PCs

What is a Tablet PC?

The Tablet PC is a fully functional portable computer that can be operated with a digital pen. The pen can be used to 'write' on the screen.

Handwriting recognition technology enables users to create handwritten documents. These can be converted into typed text, while applications such as Windows Journal allow the user to save and search 'digital ink' documents.

Tablet PCs have been heralded by some as the future shape of technology in education. They have wireless functionality and can be used in wireless network environments.

Why use a Tablet PC?

Once they are accustomed to it, learners can find the different interface more intuitive for some tasks, and akin to using pen and paper. Tablets are easy to carry around, and can be passed between students, facilitating collaborative working. Used with wireless networks they have all the functions of a fully networked computer with the benefits of portability.

Tablets can provide a solution to some of the problems associated with access to ICT suites. They enable tutors to integrate all the known benefits of information and learning technologies (ILT) more seamlessly into the 'normal' teaching environment.

How can it be used?

- To introduce flexibility;
- to enhance collaborative working;
- to improve accessibility;
- to provide a highly portable learning environment;
- to improve handwriting;
- to encourage revision;
- to create multimedia reports;
- to improve grammar and build vocabulary.

Tablets work well across many areas of the curriculum, and specific software is available for Design, Music, Science, Physics and Maths.

Case study: Using Tablet PCs with ESOL learners

John Budis

Learners: ESOL E3a and b from a wide range of cultural backgrounds
Organisation: FE : Tower Hamlets College
Technology: Tablet PC

Aim: To develop ICT and ESOL skills by integrating ICT into Adult ESOL teaching and learning using PC tablets.

Background

There were 19 students in the class of mixed age, gender and cultural backgrounds.

The Tablets were used during 'normal' ESOL sessions where PCs were unavailable and strategies were explored to see how they could be used as 'mediational' devices and whether they assisted collaborative working. They were also used to assist the development of writing and language skills.

Learners had basic ICT skills.

Using Tablets with learners

The Tablets seemed ideal for seamlessly integrating technology into instructional and learning activities. They were used both inside and outside the classroom. Interventions were planned alongside class teaching where the class tutor was also using a Tablet. The aim was to fit in with the types of learning activities he was already using.

The Tablets were introduced on a field trip to the National Gallery. The trip started with a bus journey. The tutor had created an interactive crossword about the journey as a means of introducing the Tablet as well as developing competition between the groups sharing the Tablet. He introduced the pen, along with Windows Journal, and the more confident students were encouraged to demonstrate to others. This quickly developed a collaboration and peer support network. The top deck of the bus became a classroom, which even brought passengers into the learning situation.

On reaching the gallery, students had to find a painting they liked, describe it and record its location. Working in groups and individually, they used the Tablets to make notes and drawings.

Many of the activities used authoring suites such as Hot Potatoes (**http://hotpot.uvic.ca**) or QUIA (**http://quia.com**). These were designed to reinforce language already learned and introduce new topics. Windows Journal proved a quick and effective tool for creating electronic worksheets.

Journal

In the Stitch in Time project, students were excited when they discovered that using Journal, they could produce good quality drawings. They also loved using this program to write reports and add pictures.

Using the template function was a quick and easy way of producing electronic worksheets, and enabled the tutor to create a worksheet with spaces for students to input answers.

Findings

The Tablets worked really well in terms of integrating ICT into the curriculum, were useful teaching tools and increased learning opportunities. Both the tutors' and learners' ICT skills were enhanced as a result, even though this was not the primary goal.

Motivation

Students were highly motivated by the idea that they were trying out 'cutting edge' technology. Group work sessions generated much excitement and incidental learning. The huge variety of interactive exercises was also a motivational force.

Group work

The Tablet was very useful for stimulating group work, with all the students being proactive. This contrasted with other activities where some students preferred to work alone. Owing to limited availability, the Tablets were mostly used for group/paired activities. As a result, collaborative working and peer support developed substantially, particularly on field trips.

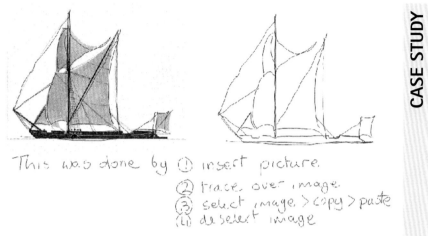

This was done by ① *insert picture.* ② *trace over image.* ③ *select image > copy > paste* ④ *deselect image*

A drawing produced in Journal.

Mobility

The portability and flexibility of Tablets enhanced the variety of locations that could be used.

Wireless networks

The wireless facility meant that the Internet could be accessed from outside the classroom. Students were able to find information for field trips and use online interactive grammar and vocabulary exercises to develop language skills.

Is the pen mightier than the mouse?

The students initially found the pen harder to use than a mouse, but thought it was more flexible.

As a teaching tool

It was easy for students to replicate activities demonstrated on the Interactive White Board (IWB). This can enhance IWB sessions (that sometimes lead the teacher back to a chalk and talk approach) making them more dynamic.

Using the pen or journal, the tutor can highlight mistakes via a data projector before giving students a printed copy.

Windows Journal allows for text, annotations, drawings and writing – all in colour. This enables ideas to be expressed and shared more effectively than text alone. Like mind mapping software, it allows for non-linear thinking, and is easier for those without touch typing skills.

Top tips

1. Ensuring that wireless technology devices work properly takes more time than conventional ICT.
2. Ensure adequate time has been allocated to plan and introduce.
3. Involve technical support from start.
4. Do a test run before class starts.
5. Encourage students to work in groups, and design work accordingly.

Resources

- ■ Tablet PC
- ■ Internet access
- ■ Planned activity

Teaching strategies

Collaboration

The students enjoyed working in pairs and groups. Discussions were often as much to do with finding more effective ways to operate the Tablet as with the task in hand. Peer teaching was much in evidence and students enjoyed sharing and watching others try before having a go. This allowed confidence building both for learning ICT skills and performing the set tasks. Interaction amongst and between groups of learners was remarkable. Crosswords worked particularly well with group work.

On many occasions, students used a combination of learning tools alongside the Tablet; e.g. electronic translators, paper dictionaries, class vocabulary lists, worksheets. One of the many projects students participated in was A Stitch In Time. This had the goal of creating a tapestry on a chosen theme. Journal can be used to trace images and then copy the tracings on to a blank worksheet; when coloured, these produced dramatic effects.

Autonomy

The various ways a Tablet can be used aided independent working. Students who wanted to continue working on tasks once the lesson was over were allowed to take Tablets home, resulting in a noticeable improvement in skills.

When using them on field trips, students were keen to explore the ability to annotate worksheets and incorporate their digital photos into reports.

Variety

Tutors were able to take advantage of all the Internet resources and those on the college's own intranet. The ability to create differentiated worksheets and make them accessible to students in the classroom or canteen was a big advantage. The richness and variety of the resources helped maintain student interest and enhance their learning. Musical gap-fills, quizzes and crosswords were all used to this effect.

Artefacts

The drawings, handwritten notes and reports created by students were of a very high standard, and students were keen to improve and update them and to get colour print-outs.

I like cutty Sark the most. because it's a beautiful ship. It's had very good shape.

Writing on Tablet on a field trip.

Useful links

Evaluation of the Tablet PC in schools:
> http://www.publications.becta.org.uk/display.cfm?resID=25889
> http://www.futurelab.org.uk/resources/publications_reports_articles/
> web_articles/web_article527

Case studies/research:
> MIT: http://icampus.mit.edu/projects/tabletpc.shtml
> Aberdeen: http://www.bgfl.org/services/elearn/tabletpc.htm
> BGfL: http://www.bgfl.org/services/editaal/projects.htm

Resources for education:
> http://www.microsoft.com/windowsxp/tabletpc/evaluation/
> bymarket/education/default.mspx

Tools:
> http://www.microsoft.com/windowsxp/downloads/powertoys/
> tabletpc.mspx
> http://www.microsoft.com/windowsxp/tabletpc/evaluation/
> about.mspx

5 | Using online games in family learning

What are online games?

Online games are readily accessible on the Internet. They vary from card games and puzzles to complex adventure games, and are aimed at a range of audiences.

Many websites (e.g. the BBC) provide educational games which we would recommend using with *Skills for Life* learners.

Why use online games?

Some games enable adult learners to practise skills in a fun, interactive way and provide immediate feedback, while others build on problem-solving skills and encourage collaboration and peer support. Other uses for online games:

- differentiation of learner activity – selecting games that cover their skills need (or their child's needs);
- to meet learning styles;
- to improve problem-solving skills;
- to encourage collaboration and peer support;
- to initiate discussion;
- to identify areas of need – informal assessment.

How can they be used?

Assessment

Online games can be used to assess learning and skills levels in a non-threatening way. They provide learners with the opportunity to see their progress while identifying to the tutor areas for further development.

Consolidation and revision of skills

Online games provide an opportunity for learners to make sure they have grasped skills/knowledge and can apply them in different contexts. Certain games can also provide a good means of revising.

Ice-breaker activities

Games are often used as ice-breakers and to help with group dynamics. They could be proposed as a whole-group activity, but splitting classes into teams can add a degree of competition, providing opportunities for discussion and peer support.

Case study: Online games used to develop mental maths skills within family learning

Sally Betts

Learner: Parent/Carers in Family Learning

Organisation: Portsmouth City Council's Adult and Community Learning (ACL) Family Learning Literacy and Numeracy Programmes

Level: Numeracy Entry 3 – Level 1

Technology: Using online games

Aim: to provide parents with the skills and strategies to help their children through the Key Stage 2 Mental Maths Test. Online games were used to facilitate this, with an emphasis on making maths fun, promoting autonomous learning and fostering a desire to share numeracy learning activities with their children.

Background

A one-day workshop was delivered to parents of Year 5 children in partnership with Fernhurst Primary School, Portsmouth. The school wished to focus on their Year 5 children, who were about to begin preparation for their Key Stage 2 SATs. The workshop was focused on the mental maths test, which allowed different strategies to be explored for addition, subtraction, multiplication and division, the last two having proved problematic for the children.

Using online games with learners

The tutor was unaware of the skills levels of the parents or the numbers to expect, so she aimed it towards Entry 3 / Level 1. The aims were:

■ to raise awareness of strategies children use to perform calculations, providing opportunities to practise these in a supported environment;

■ to show opportunities that ICT offers as an information and learning tool;

■ to provide ICT skills to enable further autonomous learning.

Discussion

The session began with a discussion about their children's numeracy work and parents' existing knowledge of the Key Stage 2 Tests. They spoke openly about their children's skills and their own Internet experience.

Assessment

In order to identify those parents with numeracy skills needs, some assessment activities were carried out. The first was the paper-based Basic Skills Initial Assessment Version 3. The second was the BBC's online Revisewise Key Stage 2 Mental Maths Test.

The mental maths test initiated many discussions. Findings included:

- parents did not realise their children had to take a mental maths test;
- they were surprised at how difficult the test was;
- they themselves had problems answering the questions;
- all decided to use it to help their children practise.

The online test also enabled the tutor to observe parents as they used the computer, providing further information about their ICT-skills levels. All were able to log on by following verbal instructions, and they knew how to access the Internet.

The session: Using the Internet to play games

Because of the existing skill levels of the parents, strategies for adding and subtracting could be covered quickly. The parents were introduced to the BBC Revisewise website. They used the online learning modules, factsheets and worksheets to explore strategies. The online modules were well received, and gave the tutor a further opportunity to observe them.

Multiplication and division

More time was spent on multiplication and division, as this was identified as a skill weakness amongst the parents. Following a discussion about the way people learn, the tutor used the 9-times table to get them to look at different strategies to help with:

- patterns in tables;
- near number;
- doubling and halving;
- partitioning (the grid method);
- using flip cards.

The website **http://www.multiplication.com** provided an opportunity for them to select two multiplication tables that they could print out in order to produce flip cards – one appropriate for their child and the other for themselves.

The games

The parents were provided with addresses for free online numeracy games. As they accessed the websites, the tutor gave them individual support.

Parents were then encouraged to play games of their choice. They were shown how to produce their own web guide to games they felt to be of value.

Findings

The games were far more successful than expected.

- Parents became so engaged that they invited others to compete with them, generating a lot of discussion.
- They practised skills at levels which they themselves found taxing, rather than at their child's level.

CASE STUDY

- Many of the games were timed, which meant that players had to use efficient strategies. When they got stuck, the game would time out, giving the tutor an opportunity to discuss alternative strategies and encouraging group discussion and collaboration.
- The activity allowed differentiation, as parents could look at any game, regardless of skill.
- Parents, in turn, discovered games that covered skills that had not been planned for, such as working with angles.

On evaluating the workshop, the tutor identified the importance of having access to an IT suite for any future family numeracy courses. The use of online games provided an opportunity to practise skills, as well as aiding teaching and helping learners to develop autonomy.

Top tips

1. Parents should complete an ICT questionnaire in advance.
2. Have an initial meeting with the school to find out their particular needs. In that way the school recognises the benefit to them and will support the workshop.
3. Find out if the school itself uses online games with the children and what they are.
4. Encourage parents to model strategies, in order to show there is more than one way to reach an answer.
5. Encourage parents to share good games they find.
6. Although you can direct parents initially to good games, let them find their own level and move freely to other games. They can naturally differentiate their own learning needs.

Resources

- Computers with Internet access
- List of game websites
- Planned activities

Teaching strategies

ICT was used within the workshop in a number of different ways, each time with a specific purpose in mind.

- Online assessment was used to:
    - assess the adults' mental maths skills;
    - provide some assessment, through observation, of their ICT skills;
    - simulate a real mental maths test to aid parents' understanding of the expectations of their child (skills and methodology).

- The internet was used to:
    - promote autonomous learning;
    - practise strategies (modelled above);
    - provide fun opportunities for shared learning to parent/child;
    - provide up-to-date and relevant information;
    - provide non-ICT resources that could facilitate parent/child learning.

Collaboration

Whilst demonstrating/modelling strategies and playing the online games, the parents collaborated and supported each other. There was a lot of sharing and competition.

Autonomy

The use of online games gave parents the opportunity to decide what skill they practised and at what level. The production of a web book enabled them to access the games at home with their children. Websites such as the BBC's were shown to have areas for their own skill development too.

Variety

The games provided an opportunity to practise strategies covered in the workshop. Stopping parents whilst they used them gave the tutor the chance to have group discussions and an opening to teach new skills or extend existing ones. In some cases, the games were used for formative assessment and as activities within the joint session.

Artefacts

The learners produced web books of websites/games they felt would benefit their children.

Useful links (maths)

Covers all areas of maths but has a section on addition, subtraction, multiplication and division called 'The Number Monster':
http://www.coolmath-games.com

Provides its own games and links to other games websites:
http://www.woodlands-junior.kent.sch.uk/maths/index.html

Other paper-based games to print out and do with a child:
http://www.adrianbruce.com/maths/index.htm

Interactive games, flashcards and worksheets:
http://www.aplusmath.com

Any of the activities can be used once the correct level has been found:
http://www.rainforestmaths.com

Links to many educational online games: http://www.topmarks.co.uk

This banana hunt game, found by one parent, helps to visualise angle sizes. Parents competed to gain the highest score;
http://www.oswego.org/ocsd-web/games/bananahunt/bhunt.html

6 | Web Quests

What is a Web Quest?

A Web Quest is an interactive learning activity using predominantly Internet resources. It provides learners with a structured way of using the Internet within lessons, enabling them to focus on assimilating information instead of spending time looking for sites.

Web Quests contain the following sections: Introduction, Task, Process, Resources, Evaluation/Conclusion. They usually consist of HTML pages and can be created with authoring software such as FrontPage and Webpage Wizard. However, most are constructed either by using a Web Quest generator (e.g. **http://aclresources.net/Webquests/**) or by saving a Word document/s as a webpage to an individual computer or network.

Why use a Web Quest?

Web Quests are based on the ideas of being inquisitive and constructive, and can help learners develop research, writing, problem-solving and presentational skills.

They are useful for topic-based or investigative-style activities, which provide open-ended questions and require learners to develop creative and problem-solving skills. They can also help to develop social and collaboration skills.

A Web Quest can be used in the classroom or accessed from outside, making it very versatile.

How can it be used?

Web Quests have been used with a wide range of learners from Entry 1 to postgraduate, and can be with individual or collaborative working in mind. Some Web Quests require students to perform different roles.

They can be dipped into, providing links to activities to consolidate learning, or provide a self-standing project which incorporates a number of learning objectives (e.g. handling money, extracting information and using time in a project called Planning a Trip).

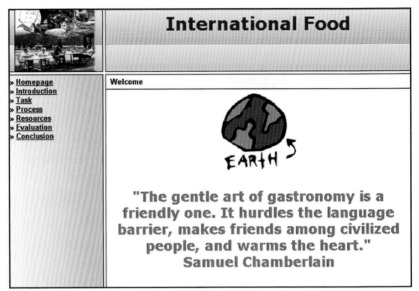

International Food

» Homepage
» Introduction
» Task
» Process
» Resources
» Evaluation
» Conclusion

Welcome

EARTH

"The gentle art of gastronomy is a friendly one. It hurdles the language barrier, makes friends among civilized people, and warms the heart."
Samuel Chamberlain

Example Web Quest – International food.

Web Quests have been used for revision. Learners have created their own Web Quests with links to specific sites they intend to use. This idea has proved successful with literacy and ESOL learners.

Case study: Web Quests with Entry 1 ESOL learners

CASE STUDY

Frieda Marti-Collett and Cathy Clarkson

Learners: ESOL Entry 1
Organisation: FE – Dewsbury College
Technology: Web Quest

Aim: To develop learners' language and ICT skills and encourage collaborative and independent learning through the use of Web Quests.

Background

The groups consisted of two ESOL Entry 1 classes meeting five times a week. The programme was flexible, but a minimum attendance of three sessions was required. These were delivered by a personal tutor. The scheme of work for each class was developed by their personal tutor and the language focus and skills for the IT and option classes followed on from this. The scheme of work for the classes changed little throughout the project. The personal tutors and the IT tutors worked together to maintain coherence between the lessons' language and the IT focus.

Using Web Quests with learners

The Entry 1 ESOL scheme of work included a variety of topics associated with the level's language outcomes (e.g. My Day, My Week, Shopping, Likes and Dislikes, etc).

The groups had previously carried out work on the computer and Internet and were confident finding information.

A Web Quest generator was used to create the 'Shopping' Web Quest, which was used as part of a blended teaching session over two weeks. The tasks set within the Web Quest were aimed at reinforcing previously practised IT/language skills.

The session was introduced using a data projector and the structure of the Web Quest demonstrated. The group was then split into pairs and worked together discussing and setting themselves individual roles in order to accomplish specified tasks.

The first was to write a shopping list. The groups explored several supermarkets before choosing where to buy their goods. Worksheets were completed containing the name of the item, the price and a picture. Learners then used their notes to create a PowerPoint presentation, which was used as an *aide-memoire* when presenting their shopping search results orally to the group. The results from the different groups were compared to identify best-buys.

During the exercise speaking and listening, reading for specific information, detail and vocabulary skills were developed.

In the final term, learners were presented with a three-week project on planning a trip. A Web Quest **http://www.aclresources.net/inroadstrip/index.html** was mixed with a treasure hunt, train times and weather forecast. The mini-project concluded with a writing task – a diary of the trip.

The various steps involved in completing the two quests allowed learners to practise and reinforce language points previously covered with their personal tutor, and create their own content.

CASE STUDY

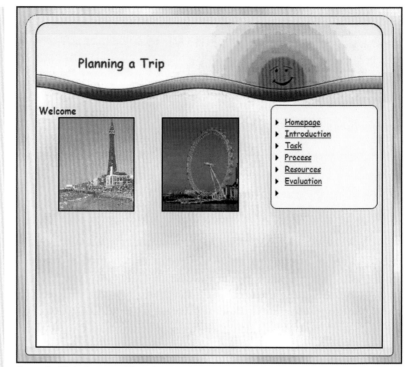

Example Web Quest – Planning a trip.

The findings

The time spent preparing the first Web Quest is rewarded by having an excellent resource which can be used again and again, providing a resource for students to take control of their own learning and work collaboratively, even at Entry 1.

The skills demonstrated by the learners exceeded what was expected at this level. They navigated sites, completed and printed electronic-based worksheets, made paper-based notes and then compared orally their shopping search results, all the while working in pairs/groups, discussing and setting themselves roles. Learners proved capable of obtaining relevant information even with an imperfect command of the language.

Another challenging aspect of the project was finding suitable websites for Entry 1 ESOL learners. This was overcome by using local and familiar websites in which the learners had to find information such as opening times, prices, courses and sports.

The learners found Web Quests motivating because they were using sites that were relevant to them. Attendance improved, students arrived early, and there was much interaction between learners.

Top tips

1. Plan out the task carefully before selecting the websites.
2. Make sure your learners are familiar with Internet browsing and have the necessary technical skills before giving them the first Web Quest.
3. Use the Web Quest with another tutor so that you can share/support each other.
4. Regularly check on the currency of the websites, as content can change frequently.

Resources

- Computers and Internet connection
- Web Quest activity and associated resources e.g. worksheets
- http://www.aclearn.net
- http://ferl.qia.org.uk/display.cfm?resID=6110
- http://webquest.sdsu.edu

Teaching strategies

Collaboration and autonomy

The Web Quests were created not only to develop learners' language and ICT skills but also to encourage collaborative and independent learning. The use of peer support and collaborative working were planned as teaching strategies.

Lesson delivery was planned with minimal tutor demonstration or handouts. The challenge for learners was to support each other in order to complete tasks.

At the start, it was difficult for learners to rely less on their tutor, but as their confidence increased, they became more independent and collaborative. After completing their first Web Quest, they were more familiar with its structure, and were observed supporting each other more frequently during the second quest.

CASE STUDY

Web Quests engage learners and decentralise learning, with students gaining more autonomy and awareness of their own learning skills. To this end, tutors should refrain from providing instant answers.

Web Quests require learners to apply and synthesise knowledge – to engage in active learning, as well as reading and remembering. Learners also practise listening and speaking skills as they work with partners or present to large groups.

Artefacts

Learners using the 'Shopping' and 'Planning a Trip' Web Quests completed electronic worksheets and diaries and created PowerPoint presentations.

Useful links

http://ferl.qia.org.uk

http://www.webquestuk.org.uk/index.htm

http://webquest.sdsu.edu

http://www.thirteen.org/edonline/concept2class/webquests/index_sub7.html

http://www.aclearn.net

http://ferl.qia.org.uk/display.cfm?resID=6110

http://www.teach–nology.com/web_tools/web_quest/

http://www.call–esl.com/samplewebquests/webquestcontents_htm.htm

http://www.grammarmancomic.com/wquestmenu.html

7 Using social networking

What is social networking?

Social networking refers to a category of Internet applications to help connect
friends, business partners or other individuals together using a variety of tools
(Wikipedia: **http://www.wikipedia.com**).

Social networking can be carried out using a variety of applications such as
blogs, wikis, podcasting or videoblogs, as well as social networking websites such
as MySpace. These sites are very popular with young adults, who use them as a
means of communicating within their peer group. They allow users to create a
personal profile and usually have privacy controls that allow the user to choose
who can view their profile or contact them.

Why use social networking?

- To create a personalised space where learners can upload content (photos,
  messages, blog posts, videos, quizzes, polls) and communicate with other
  members, including the tutor.
- To encourage interaction between learners inside and outside the classroom.

How can it be used?

Information-sharing features such as blogs and wikis can be used to develop
language, literacy and numeracy skills:

- Blogs (weblogs, or diaries) can develop reading and following written
  instructions; writing narratives, diary, record of work, peer-marking, proof
  reading.
- Quizzes (created by the learners or the tutor) can develop literacy/numeracy,
  and for initial assessment.
- Photo albums provide opportunities for descriptive writing, narratives and
  group discussion.
- Polls can be used for initial assessment; learners' opinions about various
  topics, as well as group discussions.

- All these features provide networking opportunities between group members.

- Learners can create and upload their own video, creating stories within family learning, developing interviewing techniques or writing and describing their own country and experiences.

Case study: Using a social network website with ESOL learners

Frieda Marti–Collett

Learners: ESOL E3
Organisation: Dewsbury College (FE)
Technology: Social network website – **http://www.bebo.com**

Aim: To promote independent learning and peer collaboration, and to improve learners' English writing skills by using a social network website.

Background

The learners

The group comprised ten women who attended part-time ESOL outreach classes three times a week. The programme consisted of two ESOL sessions and one CALL (Computer Assisted Language Learning) session. The CALL classes were timetabled in a room containing ten PCs.

The scheme of work for each class was developed by their personal tutor and the language focus and skills for the CALL classes followed on from this. The personal tutor and ESOL tutor worked together to maintain coherence between the lessons' language and IT focus.

Although sharing the same ESOL level (E3), some learners were absolute beginners in terms of ICT, while others had good ICT knowledge. Five learners had been attending CALL classes for two years, while the other five were new to this type of lesson and to computers.

Objectives

The main objectives were to test the effectiveness of one of the social networking websites in terms of promoting independent learning, peer collaboration and improving English writing skills. Taking learning outside the classroom and learners being able to communicate with each other was also an aim.

What we did

Choosing a network

The first step was to introduce and discuss with the learners the concept of social networks and to give them the opportunity to choose between two websites (**http://www.bebo.com** and **http://www.gazzag.com**). To make this possible, personal accounts were created for learners on both sites.

The class was split in groups of three and their task was to sign in and navigate the sites in order to complete a paper-based website comparison worksheet. At the end of the lesson, they chose Bebo, because it was easier to navigate and offered more features/resources.

Creating a social network of learners

The next step was to invite learners to join a previously created Bebo page. The process of accepting a Bebo invitation for the first time leads to the creation of a personal page and a profile. The learners had a good opportunity to practise writing about themselves and their likes and dislikes, and one lesson was devoted to that.

All learners then appeared in the Bebo page as 'Friends', and the tutor appeared in their webpages. All were able to access each other's pages by clicking on the profile picture or username. During the follow-up lesson, learners invited other learners to join their own sites and accepted each other's invitations, creating a social network.

Social networks tasks

The learners' first ESOL/Bebo activity was a Chinese New Year quiz which was created in My Page. Their task, working in pairs, was to sign in to their Bebo pages and check the internal mail which contained instructions for them to access webpages about the topic.

Having completed the quiz, they could check their scores and add a comment. This lesson was so successful, and the learners so enjoyed the quiz, that they asked if they could write their own.

The *photo* area of the website was used in various ways. One group activity involved copying a chosen photo from the tutor's album to their albums and using it to write a story. Another was to take and upload photographs of the community centre and use them in a PowerPoint presentation.

Extract from session plan.

Content	Language focus	IT focus	Resources	Assessment
Social network comparison	Reading – locate info	**http://www.bebo.com** **http://www.gazzog.com**	Computer, printer, disks, paper, whiteboard H01	Locate organisational features such as contents, index, menus, and understand their purpose (Rt/E3.5a).
Social network – Bebo	Reading – complete online forms	Opening email, setting up social network account	Computer, printer, disks, paper, whiteboard, **http://www.bebo.com**	Locate and use organisational features such as contents, index, menus, and understand their purpose (Rt/E3.5a, Rt/E3.5b) Record information on forms.
Festivals and celebrations – the Chinese New Year	Reading, finding specific information (scanning), new vocabulary	Enter web address, web navigation, social network – Quiz of the Day!	Computer, printer, disks, paper, whiteboard, **http://www.new-year.co.uk/chinese history.htm** **http://www.factmonster.com/spot/chinesenewye ar1.html**	Scan different parts of text to locate information (Rt/E3.7a)

continued overleaf

Extract from session plan (continued).

Content	Language focus	IT focus	Resources	Assessment
The Weekly News	Reading comprehension, making questions – quiz	Bebo quiz page	Computer, printer, disks, paper, whiteboard, **http://www.bebo.com**	Extract the main points and ideas, and predict words from context (Rt/E3.4a). Use punctuation to aid clarity in relation to beginnings and ends of sentences (Ws/E3.3a)
The Weekly News – Part 2	Reading news, answering questions	Bebo quiz page	Computer, printer, disks, paper, whiteboard, **http://www.bebo.com**	Scan different parts of text to locate information (Rt/E3.7a)
Photo stories	Writing short composition based on photos: direct speech, adjectives	Using Bebo photo album	Computer, printer, disks, paper, whiteboard, **http://www.bebo.com**	Plan and draft writing (Wt/E3.1b). Structure main points of writing in short paragraphs (Wt/E3.2a).

CASE STUDY

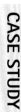

CASE STUDY

3) What is the Chinese New Year also known as?
a) Yan Tang *(0)*
b) The Spring Festival ✓ *(6)*
c) The Lunar New Year *(1)*
d) The Solar New Year *(0)*
e) Happy New Year *(0)*

100% I rearly like quiz.
The quiz are fun I very enjoied.

60% This quiz is very hard for me because i didn,t read it properly.

4) When do preparations for the festival begin?
a) 15 days before the New Year. *(0)*
b) The night before the New Year. *(2)*
c) Two weeks before the New Year. *(0)*
d) One month from the date of the Chinese New Year.
   ✓ *(5)*
e) Seven days before the New Year. *(0)*

100% I like this quiz.I am intarestring make this quiz.Icant riding fast but ilike this quiz.

Illustration from Bebo (names removed).

The *blog* area was used to give a lesson introduction to the learners and instructions about the tasks. Most used this space as a work diary, where they described the CALL lessons and their opinions about how it went.

Findings

The pedagogical nature of social network websites could be associated to social constructivism, as learning is viewed as the process by which learners are integrated into a knowledge community. The setting up of a social network website community gave learners a sense of belonging and ownership, which was an important motivational factor.

The learners provided feedback by answering six questions created in the poll area of the tutor's Bebo page. In general, they felt more confident with their English writing skills than their IT skills.

Communication between network members and creation of content was happening outside the classroom, and peer collaboration was important with regards to the motivation and support of the new learners and completion of the language tasks.

The establishment of a social network using this type of website can be time-consuming, especially when there is an attendance issue. Even the initial sending and receiving of invitations took more weeks than expected, due to learners' absences.

However, using the tool had such a positive impact that some learners still sent messages to their tutor and created content in their pages after the sessions had finished.

▶ ## Do you feel more confident writing in English?

336 da
a

a) yes   85%

b) no   0%

c) I don't know   14%

Delete | 7 Votes | 0 Comment

▶ ## Has using Bebo helped you with your English writing skills?

336 da
a

a) yes   100%

b) yes, a little   0%

c) not as much as I expected   0%

d) no   0%

e) not at all   0%

Delete | 7 Votes | 0 Comment

Extract from Bebo page.

Top tips

1. Read the safety pages on the site that you are intending to use and make sure you use the privacy setting to limit access to the site to your group.

2. You may want to experiment with a social network website before using it. Set one up and invite friends, relatives or colleagues to join.

3. Try out as many resources as possible (wiki, blogs, quizzes etc.).

4. Make sure your learners know about the advertising on the site (provided by the sponsors) and not to click on any advertising links/images.

5. Check with your organisation that they do not block access to social network sites. You may need to negotiate to get access for learners.

Resources

- Computers and Internet connection
- Registration to Bebo or similar social networking website
- Planned activities integrating social networking into sessions

Teaching strategies

Collaboration

One of the main reasons for having chosen this group of learners for the project was the fact that collaboration had been observed many times since the beginning of the academic year.

The more IT-experienced learners used to sit next to and support first-time users. This supportive environment was an important first step when introducing the concept of social network and subsequent activities, which were planned to promote and reinforce collaboration. Tutor demonstration and handouts were restricted in order to encourage learners to experiment with the technology.

For most of the new learners, it was difficult not to rely so much on their tutor, but with the support of the other learners and their own growing confidence, they became more independent and collaborative as the year progressed.

Autonomy

The use of this technology not only permitted collaborative classroom activities but also enabled learners to extend their learning outside the classroom and work at home or wherever Internet access was available. Learners' independent use of the social network included:

- uploading family photos to their albums and writing comments in each others' albums;
- writing stories in their blogs;
- leaving messages on the whiteboard;
- creating quizzes;
- uploading favourite videos.

Variety and artefact

Bebo's diversity of features was a great advantage when planning language and IT activities. Learners not only developed their Internet browsing skills, but also:

- used digital cameras;
- uploaded photos to their albums;
- created PowerPoint presentations with their own pictures;
- pasted images from other learners' and the tutor's albums;
- posted stories to their blogs.

The writing activities Bebo enabled peer-marking and sharing of experiences and skills. Learners were able to create a personalised space for themselves where they could upload their own content and communicate with others, including the tutor, at any time.

Useful links

Other social network websites:

http://www.multiply.com

http://www.friendster.com

http://www.myspace.com

http://www.facebook.com

http://www.gazzag.com

http://www.passado.com

8 Voting technology

What is voting technology?

Voting technology is used in television programmes such as 'Test the Nation' and 'Who Wants to be a Millionaire?'

Electronic voting systems consist of handsets and computer software. Interactive quizzes and questions are projected on to a screen, and by selecting a button on their handset, learners can respond to questions. The answers are recognised by the voting system, which stores the responses, and can display the results in graph form, or provide detailed statistics and reports for the tutor.

Why use voting technology?

- to provide a non-threatening means of delivering assessments;
- to make assessing learning fun;
- to save time marking paper-based assessments;
- to have evidence of progression;
- to provide immediate feedback on class/learner skills in order to adapt lessons;
- to provide learners with instant access to their results;
- to improve accessibility – no writing involved.

How can it be used?

- *Assessment* – It is ideally used as an initial and formative assessment tool, but can also be used for summative assessment.
- *Evaluation* of teaching/training sessions can easily be carried out using the system.
- *Interaction* – when the voting pads are used one per group instead of individually, speaking and listening, and group discussion skills can be developed.
- *Surveys* – to find out from potential learners what they would like to study and how.

- *Promotion* – Plymouth and Portsmouth Adult and Community Learning staff have used electronic voting technology to carry out a 'Test the City' event using a quiz based on local history, literacy and numeracy, and as a means of advertising local learning opportunities. Plymouth's case study can be found on **http://www.aclearn.net**.

- *Community Engagement* – holding competitions across community/school groups

Systems available

Voting technology systems available include:

- Quizdom
- TurningPoint
- Activote
- PPvote

Case study: Voting technologies for assessment

Sally Betts, Jo Duckett and Elaine Husselby

Learners: Parent/Carers in Family Learning
Organisation: Portsmouth City Council's Adult and Community Learning
                (ACL) Family Learning Literacy and Numeracy Programmes
Technology: Voting Technologies (PPVote), laptop and digital projector

Aim: To explore how assessment in family learning can be carried out using voting technologies.

Background

Portsmouth City Council's ACL Family Learning Literacy and Numeracy Programmes are delivered in family learning or community rooms in schools. Tutors have highlighted initial assessment of learners as an area for improvement. Previously they had used paper-based tests, but they wanted to find a quick and fun way of assessing learners that would also reduce marking time.

It was decided to trial voting technologies for initial assessment and, on the shorter courses, for final assessment also. The hope was that by testing throughout the programme, they would find a more effective way of tracking progress and achievement, in line with the Recognising and Recording Progress and Achievement (RARPA) requirements for non-accredited learning.

CASE STUDY

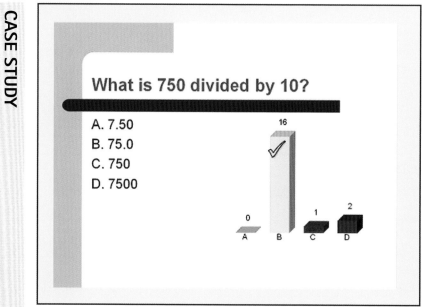

Question and results.

Using voting technology with learners

The voting technologies were used to assess the parents initially on the topic area to be covered during that particular session; e.g. shape, basic calculations and percentages.

After each question, the learners viewed the class results on a graph with the correct answer highlighted. This led to discussion between learners. Where the majority answered a question incorrectly, the tutor told them they would cover the topic in more detail later. Seeing the answers during the test fostered peer support.

The assessment data was exported to Excel and the results displayed as a PowerPoint presentation. This provided evidence of progression and achievement for each learner, which could then be discussed with them. All tutors appreciated the instant results, and the removal of the chore of processing individual papers.

At the end of the course, questions from the previous weeks' initial assessments that had caused problems were added to the final course assessment to find out whether learners had retained knowledge.

Findings

The learners

The learners required very little training to use the handsets, which were no harder to use than a TV remote control.

There was a far more relaxed atmosphere for assessments delivered in this way. Most learners were very positive about using the technology, saying that they would rather be assessed by this method than a paper-based test. However, when taking numeracy assessments, they wanted access to pen and paper to do their working out. Learners were also not sure that they wanted to do an accredited assessment in this way because of the inability to go back and review any questions about which they were unsure. This important issue needs to be considered.

Using the technology

The tests were not timed, although the software allows for timing. The tutors moved on to the next question once every learner had voted. They discussed what to do when one learner was taking a long time to answer, and decided to stay with non-timed tests, but to tell the learners when they were about to ask the next question.

The amount of information gained by the tutor was greater than with paper-based tests. Because the learners look up at a screen, the tutor is able to see their reactions as they read the question, see how long it takes them to answer and observe their reactions when the answers are shown. Tutors found that this informed their teaching, making them aware of which learners needed more support. Learners' remarks on seeing the answers enabled tutors to open up discussions and use the assessment as a learning opportunity.

Learner comments about using the handsets for accredited tests:

It would be fine – it would take the pressure off as on paper you can keep reading and re-reading – changing answers and think too much!

Handsets make you relax and concentrate only on the question at hand.

Great to use technology. However, no control to go back and check answers – no independence waiting for the rest of the group or vice versa.

The tutors

Tutors required time to master the software, but once they had made one assessment, they found it simple. They gave each other peer support, producing assessments together and visiting each other's classrooms to provide support when the system was first used.

The tutors found that creating the assessments took time initially, but they recognised that they could be used over and over again. Initially, they spent a lot of time finding images to go with each question, but soon realised that these made no difference to the learners' experience, simply cluttering the screen.

The tutors have all agreed that using voting technologies was their preferred method of assessment. They are now looking at other uses, such as course evaluation, and plan to hold an inter-schools 'Ask the Family' competition.

Top tips

1. Plan sufficient time to learn the software, make assessments and become confident in using the technologies. Set up peer support mechanisms.

2. If the software does not work as expected, speak to the manufacturer.

3. Make one assessment that covers all the course sessions and hide questions not needed that week.

4. Have a practice question for learners who are using the sets for the first time before actually starting the assessment.

5. Ensure that you explain to learners that only they and the tutor will be aware of how they answered.

6. Have spare batteries for the handsets.

7. Watch your learners whilst delivering the assessment. You will learn so much.

8. If asking questions that require a number answer, be sure to use alphabetic labels e.g. a) 3, b) 4, as this reduces the risk of confusion.

Resources

- ■ PPVote, **http://www.ppvote.com**
- ■ Laptop
- ■ Data Projector
- ■ Screen
- ■ Prepared quiz/assessments

Teaching strategies

Collaboration

Because the technologies were used to individually assess learners' skills, collaboration between learners was not encouraged. However, the learners did provide peer support and peer learning between questions, and the technology did initiate discussions. It also promoted collaboration between tutors, who produced assessments together and co-delivered assessments until they were confident.

Autonomy

The system facilitated questioning by the learners.

Variety

The technologies gave tutors the opportunity to assess learners' skills by a different method than before. Although individuals were undertaking their own assessment, it felt more like a group activity. The technologies could be used in other ways during the assessment; e.g. to initiate discussion, evaluation, promotional activities and attitudinal surveys.

References

Ivanič, R and Tseng, M.-i L. (2005) *Understanding the Relationships Between Learning and Teaching: An Analysis of the Contribution of Applied Linguistics.* London: NRDC.

Kambouri, M. (2003) 'ICT and adult literacy and numeracy: observing practice', *Basic Skills Bulletin* Issue 19, Dec 2003.

Mellar, H., Kambouri, M., Wolf, A., Goodwin, T., Hayton, A., Koulouris, P. and Windsor, V. (2001) *Research into the Effectiveness of Learning through ICT for People with Basic Skills Needs.* Ufl.

Mellar, H., Kambouri, M., Sanderson, M., and Pavlou, V. (2004) *ICT and Adult Literacy, Numeracy and ESOL.* London: NRDC. Available at: **http://www.nrdc.org.uk/uploads/documents/doc_258.pdf**

Mellar, H., Kambouri, M., Logan, K., Betts, S., Nance, B. and Moriarty, V. (2007) *Effective Teaching and Learning: Using ICT.* London: NRDC.